WORLDS OF THE PAST

THE ANCIENT CHINESE

Hazel Mary Martell

new

Discovery

B·O·O·K·S

New York

First New Discovery Books edition 1993

Originally published by
HEINEMANN CHILDREN'S REFERENCE
a division of Heinemann Educational Books Ltd
Halley Court, Jordan Hill, Oxford OX2 8EJ

OXFORD LONDON EDINBURGH
MELBOURNE SYDNEY AUCKLAND
MADRID ATHENS BOLOGNA
SINGAPORE IBADAN NAIROBI HARARE
GABORONE KINGSTON PORTSMOUTH NH(USA)

© Heinemann Educational Books Ltd 1993
First Published 1993

Library of Congress Cataloging-in-Publication Data
Martell, Hazel.
    The ancient Chinese / Hazel Mary Martell.
    p.   cm. (Worlds of the Past)
    Includes index.
    Summary: Explores various aspects of ancient
Chinese culture, including art, government, societal
structure, religion, and everyday life.
    ISBN 0-02-730653-4
    1. China—Civilization—to 221 B.C.—Juvenile
literature. 2. China—Civilization—221 B.C.-960 A.D.—
Juvenile literature. 3. China—Civilization—960–1644—
Juvenile literature. [1. China—Civilization.] I. Title.
II. Series.
DS741.65.M37   1992
951'.01—dc20
                                     92-9052

Designed by Julian Holland Publishing Ltd
Cartography by Gecko Ltd
Color artwork by Fred Anderson
Picture research by Anne Marie Ehrlich
Editorial planning by Philip Steele

New Discovery Books
Macmillan Publishing Company
866 Third Avenue
New York, NY 10022

Macmillan Publishing Company is part of the
Maxwell Communication Group of Companies.

Printed in Hong Kong

93 94 95 96 10 9 8 7 6 5 4 3 2 1

Photographic acknowledgments
The author and publishers wish to acknowledge, with
thanks, the following photographic sources:
Ancient Art and Architecture Collection pp49, 59*al*;
British Museum pp16*ar*, 42*ar*, 46*ar*, 54; C M Dixon
pp5*ar*, 14, 36; E T Archive pp9, 12, 15*al*, 15*br*, 20, 28,
35*al*, 37, 39, 41*bl*, 42*bl*, 43, 48, 57; Sally and Richard
Greenhill pp7*al*, 23*b*, 25*al*, 25*br*, 27, 32, 44, 50; Robert
Harding Picture Library pp5*br*, 6, 18, 19*al*, 24, 26, 30*ar*,
45*al*, 46*ar*, 52, 53, 55, 59*br*; Michael Holford pp21*br*,
29*r*, cover(*al*) and 40, 45*br*, 51; Hutchison Library pp11,
33*al*, 35*br*; Photo Hubert Josse title page, pp7*br*, 13;
MacQuitty Collection pp21*al*, 22, 23*a*; Werner Forman
Archive pp16*bl*, 19*br*, 29*l*, 30*bl*, 34, cover(*bl*) and 38,
58; Werner Forman Archive/Art Gallery of New South
Wales, Australia pp26, cover(*r*) and 56; Werner
Forman Archive/British Library pp8; Werner Forman
Archive/Gerald Godfrey, Hong Kong p31; Werner
Forman Archive/Peking Palace Museum p17; Werner
Forman Archive/Sotheby's, London p33*br*; Zefa
pp41*ar*, 47.
a = above, b = below, c = center, l = left, r = right
The publishers have made every effort to trace the
copyright holders, but if they have inadvertently
overlooked any, they will be pleased to make the
necessary arrangements at the first opportunity.

Note to the reader
In this book there are some words in the text that are printed in **bold** type. This shows that the word is listed in the glossary
on page 62. The glossary gives a brief explanation of words that may be new to you.

Contents

Who were the Ancient Chinese?   4
How we know about them   6
Evidence from words and pictures   8
From hunting to farming   10
Government and society   12
The "Sons of Heaven"   14
Life in a noble family   16
Warriors and mandarins   18
Life in the town   20
Life in the country   22
Food and cooking   24
Clothes and appearance   26
Faiths and beliefs   28
Funeral customs   30
Pastimes and festivals   32
Transportation   34
Trade   36
The engineers   38
The inventors   40
Writing and painting   42
Pottery and porcelain   44
Crafts and metalwork   46
Silk production   48
The early dynasties   50
Toward an empire   52
Empires and kingdoms   54
China reunited   56
The Middle Kingdom   58
Time line   60
Glossary   62
Index   64

Who were the Ancient Chinese?

The Ancient Chinese were the **ancestors** of many of the people who live in the country that we now call China. Like all early peoples, they lived at first by hunting animals and gathering seeds and berries for food. Some of these people moved around, following the animals. They were **nomads.** Other people lived in caves such as the ones at Xianrendong, which were occupied between 9000 and 5500 B.C. By about 6000 B.C. groups of people had settled and were living in villages on the banks of the Yellow River. They learned how to farm the fertile land, using stone tools. They knew how to make pottery, but they did not know how to make metals.

Evidence shows that around 3000 B.C. people had started to mine copper. This copper was mixed with small amounts of tin and lead to make **bronze.** The earliest known bronze objects in China date from 2300 B.C., by which time the Ancient Chinese had also discovered how to weave silk.

The early dynasties

The early settlers had to defend their land from those who were still nomads and from other enemies. To do this, they formed themselves

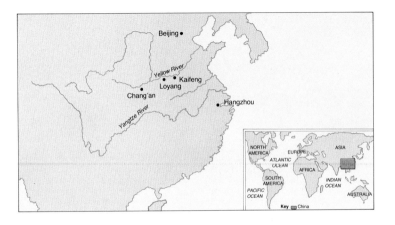

◁ The Middle Kingdom, or China, as the country was called by foreigners.

into bigger groups, made up of peoples from neighboring villages. As time passed, one family in each large group became more powerful than the others. This family ruled over its own group and soon, perhaps, over some of the neighboring families, too. Legend says that the first family, or **dynasty**, to rule over a large area was the Xia family, who came to power around 2100 B.C. There is no proof that this family ever existed, but we do know that in about 1722 B.C. the Shang dynasty took power. This dynasty lasted until 1122 B.C. and during their rule the first towns and cities were built. Bronze making became very important and a system of writing was invented.

△ A three-legged bronze bowl from the Shang dynasty. The Ancient Chinese were very practical people. As well as being inventors and engineers, they were also skilled craftworkers who made many beautiful objects that still exist today.

The Chinese empire

The Zhou dynasty followed the Shang and both were ruled by kings. However, when the Qin dynasty came to power in 221 B.C., the whole of what is now known as China was conquered and was ruled by an **emperor**. *Qin* can also be spelled "Ch'in" and it was this dynasty that gave the country the name foreigners call it, China. The Ancient Chinese used a different name, however. They called their country Zhong-Guo, which means Middle Kingdom. The Chinese people believed that their country was the center of the world and more advanced than anywhere else.

For many centuries China did lead the world in inventions, new ideas, and ways of government. Then in A.D. 1200s a Mongol army, led by Genghis Khan, conquered the north of China. His grandson, Kublai Khan, ruled over all China. The Chinese themselves did not regain control until 1368. By this time some countries in the rest of the world, such as Italy, were beginning to develop their own new ideas and inventions.

△ Later dynasties became famous for their pottery. Large amounts of fine pottery, porcelain, were made during the Sung dynasty. This wine pot and the warming-bowl are from this period.

How we know about them

People who study the buildings and objects that other people leave behind are called **archaeologists.** By digging, or **excavating,** at different sites, they have found many objects that were made and used by the Ancient Chinese. Archaeologists have made a careful study of these objects, or **artifacts,** and the places where they were found. They can then use this scientific information to build up a picture of what life was like in the past.

The earliest evidence

One of the oldest archaeological sites in China is a cave at Zhoukoudian, near Beijing. There, early humans, called Peking man, lived as long ago as 400,000 B.C. Archaeologists have found evidence of fires and stone tools at Zhoukoudian. They think that this one cave was occupied at various times for around 100,000 years. By 28,000 B.C. another cave on the site was lived in. This time the occupants were true human beings, *Homo sapiens.* Evidence shows that these people also used stone tools and lived by hunting and gathering.

Archaeologists have found more evidence of the people who settled and started farming near the Yellow River and its **tributaries.** Most of the evidence is from the site of a village called Banpo in northwest China, which was first occupied around 5000 B.C. At this site, archaeologists have found the remains of houses. The walls are made of pieces of wood, which had been split and woven together. Then mud was spread over the wood. This type of wall is called wattle and daub. The straw roofs were supported on wooden poles and the houses were round, square, or oblong in shape. The village was surrounded by a ditch. Outside the ditch was a pottery-making area and a cemetery.

△ The terra-cotta army. These life-size models of soldiers guard the tomb of Qin Shi Huangdi, the first emperor of China, who died in 210 B.C. The first figures were discovered in 1974 by farmers who were digging a well. When archaeologists excavated the site, they found over 6,000 soldiers in one pit, together with six chariots, each pulled by four horses. Most of the soldiers were infantrymen, but in a second pit more than 1,400 clay figures of horses and cavalrymen were found. They were all in formation like a real army, and archaeologists have learned a lot about warfare in Ancient China by studying the uniforms and weapons.

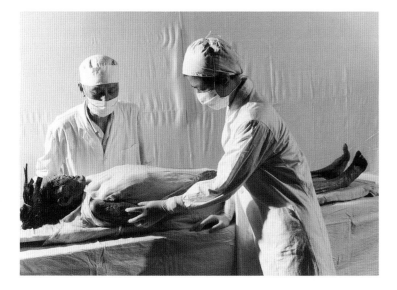

◁ Medical workers examining the body of a woman who died 2,100 years ago. When skeletons and bodies are found, archaeologists can find out how old the person was and what illnesses he or she had suffered from. They have found that many early people died from heart failure or a disease called tuberculosis.

Evidence from tombs

The best archaeological evidence is from about 1500 B.C., the period during and after the Bronze Age. By this time, important people were being buried in tombs, together with food and many of the artifacts they had used in their lives. Although most of the food has rotted away, archaeologists can still find out what it was by studying the remaining seeds and bones in a laboratory.

Archaeologists can also find out about ancient technology by studying the artifacts and finding out how they were made.

Digging up artifacts is only one part of an archaeologist's work. To make an accurate picture of Chinese life in the past, all finds must be recorded. Small finds have to be cleaned and preserved, while objects that are too big to be moved must be measured and photographed. The finds from one site can then be compared with those from another to find out how the people's way of life changed and what may have caused the changes.

△ A terra-cotta figure from the Sui dynasty of a female musician playing the lute.

7

Evidence from words and pictures

Some evidence about the life of the Ancient Chinese comes from writing or **inscriptions** that were made on bones about 3,500 years ago. These bones were used by diviners, people who try to tell the future, to answer questions put to them by the king.

The diviner took a large flat bone, such as the shoulder blade of an ox or a sheep, or the lower shell of a tortoise. The diviner then drilled some shallow pits into the surface and put a heated rod into each pit in turn. This made cracks in the bone and by looking at them, the diviner worked out the answers to the king's questions. When he had done this, he sometimes scratched both the answer and the question on the bone. The bones were called **oracle** bones because an oracle answers questions about the future.

Some of the questions were about very ordinary topics, such as the weather or how to cure a toothache. Others might ask about how to win a battle or a war. We know this because the writing on the oracle bones used small pictures, or **pictograms,** to represent each word or idea. This system is very similar to that used by the Chinese in their writing today.

△ Many oracle bones have been found in China. When they were discovered in the 19th century, they were believed to have magical properties. People called them "dragon bones" and they ground up some of the bones into powder to make cures for all sorts of illnesses. Then someone realized what the bones were and archaeologists began to study them.

The Ancient Chinese also made inscriptions on bronze containers and objects made of polished **jade.** They also wrote in ink on silk and **bamboo** and, since the first century A.D., on paper. Although silk, bamboo, and paper rot quickly, a great deal of writing has survived from early times. This includes encyclopedias, novels, poems, and histories, as well as books on medicine and religion. There are also practical books about everything from how to make war to how to make clocks.

Clues from pictures

The Ancient Chinese painted many pictures. Some of the earliest paintings have been found on the inside walls of tombs. They showed scenes from everyday life. Other pictures were made on silk **banners** that had been used at the head of funeral processions and then buried with the dead. These banners showed scenes from Chinese **legends** to explain what people believed would happen on the dead person's journey to the next world. In later dynasties landscape pictures became very popular. Many pictures have survived, showing farming and industrial scenes that tell us what Chinese technology was like at the time. Some of the pictures were painted on silk **scrolls** while others were done on paper, wood, or bamboo.

▽ A T'ang dynasty scroll of Yang Guifei, who was said to be one of the four most beautiful women in China, mounting a horse. The Emperor Minghuang was infatuated with her and finally had her murdered by angry troops.

From hunting to farming

The earliest known inhabitants of China lived more than 400,000 years ago. The best known of these early humans are called collectively Peking man, whose skulls were first discovered in northern China in 1929. Peking man used stone tools and lived by hunting and gathering. Hunting and gathering continued in China until about 6000 B.C. and even later in some areas.

By 6000 B.C., however, the first farmers had started to settle along the plain of the Yellow River. They chose this area because it is covered in a very thick layer of soil called **loess.** This fine soil is made up of small pieces or fragments that were originally carried by the wind from the edge of the Gobi Desert. The frequent flooding of the Yellow River made the soil fertile and easy to **cultivate.**

Early Yellow River farmers used better stone tools than the people who lived in caves at Zhoukoudian. These settlers built villages, such as Banpo, which had a population of around 500 people. The people in Banpo kept pigs, chickens, and dogs. They also grew a grain crop called **millet.** Millet can grow in the dry conditions that exist in that area for much of the year.

▽ A reconstruction of Banpo village, based on evidence that archaeologists found when they excavated the site. The walls of the houses were made from wattle and daub and were plastered on the inside to make them smooth. In some houses the floor was also plastered, but in others it was just bare earth. Most of the houses had a fire pit that was used for cooking and also gave heat and light.

◁ These terraces are in Guizhou Province in southern China. Agriculture was very important to the Ancient Chinese, but a lot of their land was not suitable for farming. Much of it was either too dry or too hilly. Although the soil can be very fertile it is easily blown or washed away. Over the centuries farmers have tried to stop this by building terraces on their land.

China is a vast country. Within China, different areas have different climates, so people are able to grow many different crops. For example, the southeastern Hangzhou Bay area is much warmer and wetter than Banpo, which is in northwest China. The high temperatures and heavy rainfall of the Hangzhou Bay area made it suitable for rice growing, and archaeologists have found evidence that rice was grown there by 5000 B.C. Also in that area archaeologists have found stone tools that may be hoes or **plowshares,** dating from about 3500 B.C.

The Yangshao and Longshan cultures
Toward the end of the Stone Age in China, between about 5000 and 2500 B.C., two distinct **cultures** developed in the farming settlements. The first was the Yangshao culture, which is named after a village on the Yellow River. The culture is famous for its fine pots, which were painted with geometric designs in either red or gray.

After the Yangshao came the Longshan culture, which was named after a village near China's east coast.

Government and society

The Shang and Zhou dynasties lasted from about 1700 B.C. until 221 B.C. The Zhou was the longest lived of all ruling houses in China. At this time Chinese society was ruled by a king. The king owned all the land, but he allowed members of his family and other noble families to hold parts of it. Instead of paying money to the king for the land, the nobles paid in other ways. They had to protect the land from the king's enemies and fight for the king when necessary. The noble families in turn rented their land to the **peasant** farmers, who paid for it by doing services for the nobles. Their services could include working on the nobles' land or going to war with a nobleman if the king needed men for his army. This method of paying in service instead of money to rent land is called a **feudal system.**

▽ This painting is taken from a silk scroll that dates from the T'ang dynasty, about 1,300 years ago.

◁ A silk merchant on his camel. Foreign merchants traveled to China to trade their gold for Chinese goods, such as silk and porcelain. By the time of the T'ang dynasty, merchants were coming from as far away as India and Iran to buy Chinese products to take back to their own countries. Pottery figures from this time show merchants of many different nationalities.

Society in the Chinese empire

The emperor ruled over all China. Chinese society was split into four main groups. The first group included the nobles and scholars, the *shi*. They were followed by the peasant farmers, the *nong.* The third group was the craftworkers, the *gong*, and after that came the traders, the *shang.* People in this last group were often very rich, while the peasant farmers were often very poor. However, in Ancient China, farming was said to be more important than trading, and so the poorest farmer was a more important person than the richest trader, or **merchant.**

The first emperor

In 221 B.C. Qin Shi Huangdi came to power, and the system of government changed. Qin Shi Huangdi wanted everything under his direct control. He abolished the feudal system by taking power from the nobles and making the peasants pay taxes directly to him. Qin Shi Huangdi was the first emperor of China. He ruled over more land than either the Shang or the Zhou kings had done and he wanted the same laws to be enforced everywhere. To make sure that everyone obeyed his laws, he made the punishments for disobedience harsh. These punishments included beheading, being torn apart, or being cut in half. Later emperors were usually less harsh than Qin Shi Huangdi. However, they all thought that their laws should be obeyed without questioning.

The "Sons of Heaven"

The rulers of China thought of themselves as the Sons of Heaven. This name was first used by the Zhou kings, who believed that it was heaven's wish that they rule over the country. This belief was known as the **Mandate** of Heaven. For a ruler to keep the mandate, he had to be both kind and fair. He also had to listen to his advisers, or **ministers,** and his government had to consider the welfare of the people and try to keep peace and order in the country. In return, the people had to obey their rulers.

However, not all rulers behaved as they were supposed to. Some rulers were weak or greedy, or did not protect their people by fighting China's enemies. Other rulers taxed the ordinary people very heavily to pay for building palaces, canals, roads, and walls. Sometimes these taxes were so heavy that people had to go without food in order to pay them. When that happened, people rioted and rebelled against the ruler. If they managed to overthrow the ruler, they said that heaven had taken its mandate from the emperor because he was not fit to rule. A new ruler then had the Mandate of Heaven, and a new dynasty began.

◁ A Chinese painting from a series about the beneficent governor Chao Hsai, a wise mandarin who sympathized with the people and lost office for failing to collect taxes.

◁ Qin Shi Huangdi, the first emperor, tried to destroy most of the books that had been written in the past. He did not want people to think back to old ways and ideas. This picture shows the books burning in a bonfire. The emperor also had many scholars buried alive, because their ideas were in the books. His plan was not a complete success and many books were rewritten later on.

The power of the emperor

The emperor was all-powerful. He had the power of life or death over everyone. He also had the power to make people work for him whether they wanted to or not. For example, Qin Shi Huangdi made more than 700,000 men and women work on the building of his tomb.

The emperor's way of life

From the time of the Han dynasty in 202 B.C., the emperors lived in palaces quite separate from most of their people. Government officials did most of the work of running the country, and so the emperors had a great deal of time to spend as they wished. They also went to religious ceremonies to show that they were trying to keep the Mandate of Heaven.

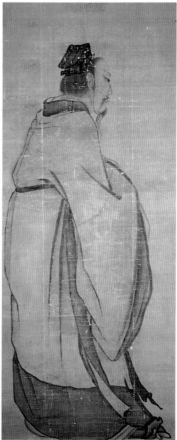

△ A portrait of the emperor Wu, who ruled China from 141–87 B.C.

Life in a noble family

After the emperor, the noble families were the next most important people in Ancient Chinese society. When China was ruled by kings, the noble families were very powerful. As part of the feudal system, they were expected to raise armies from people living on their lands to fight for the king. However, when Qin Shi Huangdi became the ruler of China in 221 B.C., he feared the noble families might use their armies to fight against him, so he abolished the feudal system. Although this took power away from the noble families, they were still very important and very rich.

Every emperor was afraid that he might lose his empire to one of the nobles. As a result, the nobles had to spend some time at the emperor's court, where he could soon find out if anyone was plotting against him. When they were not in court, however, the noble families lived in houses that were themselves like small palaces.

Most noble families owned a town house and a country estate. The town houses were usually three or four stories high, with brightly painted walls.

△ Pottery models have been found in the graves of many rich Chinese people. This model shows what a wealthy family's town house looked like. The gateway has two towers, and the upper floors have balconies. Some models even showed the courtyards with their wells or ponds. This model was made in the Han dynasty, about 2,000 years ago.

◁ This Chinese garden is very similar to those that the emperor and members of the elite enjoyed in the past. If the garden was big enough, they liked it to have lakes with small pavilions where they could sit quietly. They also liked to have lots of trees, such as weeping willows, which trailed in the water, and fruit trees, which blossomed in the spring.

The tiles on the roofs were decorated with imaginary creatures. Most houses had a courtyard with goldfish pools and potted plants, and some had trees and gardens. Inside, the houses were decorated with silk hangings and painted screens. There were many beautiful ornaments made from bronze, gold, and pottery. Some objects, such as boxes and trays, were made of wood and painted with **lacquer**.

The country estates were just as luxurious as the town properties, but they had room for more gardens, trees, and pools. To keep the family safe, each estate was surrounded by a high wall with only one gateway, usually guarded by soldiers.

Rich noble families did not work. Their income came from their estates in the country. For entertainment, the rich enjoyed large banquets at which dancers and acrobats performed. As a symbol of their noble life, both men and women started to wear silk gowns with long, flowing sleeves. This showed that they never had to do anything practical. They also grew their fingernails very long and then wore special coverings to protect them.

Foot-binding —"lily feet"

Around A.D. 970 noble Chinese families found a new way of setting their women apart from ordinary people. They decided that tiny feet were more beautiful than normal-size ones. This meant that when girls were very small, their feet were doubled up and bound tightly. This broke the bones in the arch of the foot and turned the toes under, so that the foot only grew to about half the normal length. As a result, many noblewomen could hardly walk. The fashion for "lily feet" spread throughout Chinese society and lasted until 1926. Only women who had to work on the land did not have bound feet.

◁ Wealthy women lived a life of leisure. They had servants to do all the cooking and housework and to look after the children. If their husbands had to go to the emperor's court, they would probably go, too. There they spent their time listening to music, talking, or playing games.

Warriors and mandarins

By the time of the Han dynasty, China had a large population. In the year A.D. 2, a record of all the people living in China was made. This type of record of the population is called a **census.** The census showed that there were 59,594,978 people living in China at that time. The emperor ruled over all the people, but he could not govern everything by himself. He needed many officials, or civil servants, known as mandarins, to help govern the country. The mandarins made sure that the people knew about the laws and obeyed them, and they checked that they all paid their taxes. The emperor also needed soldiers to protect him and to defend the empire from its enemies. Most emperors needed many laborers to work on large building projects, such as the Great Wall and the Grand Canal. They also forced thousands of workers to prepare huge tombs, ready for the emperor's burial when he died.

People chose a career as a civil servant, but most soldiers were forced to join the army. Any man over the age of 15 could be **conscripted**, but not all of them were. One reason for this was that

◁ Two model soldiers from the terra-cotta army in the tomb of Qin Shi Huangdi. The soldiers' weapons included knives, bows and arrows, axes, and spears. Some of our knowledge of warfare in Ancient China comes from a book written during the Zhou dynasty. Its author was a general called Sun Wu, and in the book he described how to fight wars and how to organize armies.

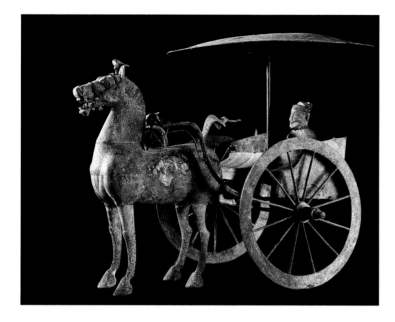

◁ Government officials traveled in style. This bronze model shows a mandarin sitting in his chariot. Transportation was provided for all the mandarins and the most important officials. The highest officials rode in fast-moving vehicles pulled by horses and driven by servants. Those who were not as important had slower carts, pulled by bullocks. Wherever they went, the officials were treated with respect. They were not allowed to work in their own districts, however, in case they were tempted to do favors for their family and friends.

the emperor needed a large army only when the empire was threatened by an enemy. For the rest of the time the young men could be more useful on their farms or working on buildings. Most forced labor work was usually done by Chinese convicts or by prisoners of war. However, during the Han dynasty, every Chinese man, apart from nobles and officials, had to work for the government for one month in every year. This work included building roads and flood barriers, laboring in the iron and salt industries, and hauling **barges** full of rice along the Grand Canal.

Mandarins and other officials

There were thousands of civil servants in Ancient China. They were all men and the most important ones, the mandarins, were close advisers to the emperor. Below the mandarins were rank after rank of officials. They ran everything, from building canals to running the iron industry, and from collecting taxes to being judges.

△ The Grand Canal today. The Grand Canal was one of the many projects built by forced labor. It was started in the reign of the second Sui emperor, Yang Ti, who ruled from A.D. 605 to 618, and it was based on a more ancient canal system. The Grand Canal linked the Yangtze River with the Huai and Yellow rivers and it is said to have taken over 2 million people to build it.

Life in the town

Although the wealth of China depended on farming, many people lived in towns and cities. The earliest towns were built on the plain of the Yellow River during the Shang dynasty, but gradually they developed all over the empire. These towns and cities were centers of trade and government, and many of them were carefully planned. Each city was surrounded by high walls. These walls were made of earth that had been poured into a wooden frame and then pressed down until it was solid. The frame was then raised to make another layer of earth on top of the first one.

Inside a walled town

Inside the main wall, the town was divided into different areas, known as **wards**. Each ward was also surrounded by a wall, with only one gate leading into it. Different groups of people lived and worked in each ward. They could go to other wards during the daytime, but at night they had to return to their own ward when a drum was

▽ Markets were busy, lively places in Ancient China.

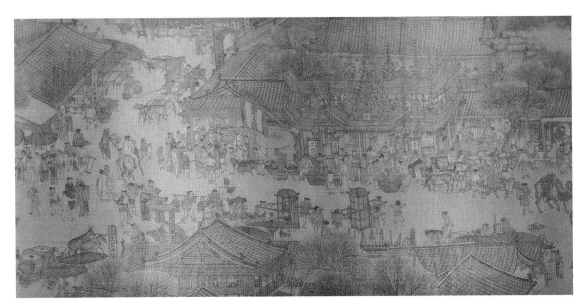

◁ Pigsties with toilets over them, as shown in this pottery model from the Han dynasty, were probably more common in the countryside than in the towns. Wherever they were found, they would be a hazard to health, as they would attract flies, which spread germs. The refuse was collected from them and used as manure to fertilize the ground for crops.

sounded. Rich people's homes had plenty of space, but in the poorer wards the houses were packed together. Poor people lived in tiny shacks made of mud walls and thatched roofs. They may have used rough curtains to keep out the drafts.

Busy streets

During the day, the streets of Chinese towns were full of people. Farmers and peasants from the surrounding countryside brought their pigs and geese, fruits and vegetables to sell in the market. Craftworkers sold beautiful objects made of jade, bronze, or lacquerware. There were also stalls selling cooked meats, soup, salt, rice, baskets, firewood, silk, and pots and pans. Some people mended wheels or made harnesses, while others offered haircuts, wrote letters, told fortunes, or begged for money or food.

All this activity took place on streets that were not paved. This meant that on dry days they were dusty and on wet days they were muddy. Piles of rotting garbage and manure lay scattered about, and in many places there were no proper drains.

△ Street entertainment was very popular in Chinese towns. Acrobats and musicians performed in the marketplaces and on street corners. Entertainment using animals was also popular.

Life in the country

Most of the Ancient Chinese people were farmers who lived in the countryside. Under the Shang and Zhou dynasties from about 1722 to 221 B.C., farmers held their land from the noble families who were their overlords. From 221 B.C., when China became an empire, the system changed. The farmers began to own the land they farmed and to pay taxes to the emperor.

This change in the system did not make life any easier for the farmers. Although most farms were small, there was enough work on each one to keep a family busy till dusk each day. Farm families usually managed to grow enough food to survive and pay their taxes. However, in times of flood, drought, or war there might be no harvest at all on some farms. If this happened, the family had to choose between starving to death or selling the land and going to work for someone else.

A farmer's year in northern China

In the cold, dry north of China, about 2,000 years ago, the main crops were wheat and millet. As winter came to an end the farmers started plowing their land. By the middle of the Han dynasty, rich farmers used ox-drawn plows. The plows had iron-tipped blades or shares and could cut deep into the soil. Poor farmers still used wooden plows that they pushed across the soil. When the land was ready, the seed was scattered on the soil by hand. Seeds for vegetables such as leeks and Chinese cabbage were sown, as well as seeds for the plant **hemp,** which provided fibers for making cloth, as well as fuel. As the crops grew, the ground had to be weeded and hoed. In dry years the crops also had to be watered throughout the summer. The fruit trees also had to be looked after. Then, if all had gone

△ Each farm had barns, granaries, and shelters for the animals. These included sheep pens, pigsties, and henhouses. This pottery model of a henhouse was buried in a tomb during the Han dynasty.

A rice farmer's year

Winter was short and summer hot in the rice-growing areas of southern China. Rice seeds were sown in special seedbeds at the start of spring. The fields were flooded and then plowed into soft mud, ready for the seedlings to be planted in May. This was done by hand and completed before the sun could dry out the seedlings. After that, the fields were kept wet for the rice to grow. When the rice ripened, the fields were drained and the crop quickly harvested. Where two crops would grow in a year, the fields were flooded and plowed again to be ready for more seedlings to be planted.

◁ Wealthy farmers' houses were often two-storied. This farmhouse is two stories high and has a tiled roof. Most of the land in China was unsuitable for cattle rearing, and so no one kept more than a couple of cows. The stone carving seen here is one of a series that show life in the countryside in Han times about 2,000 years ago.

well, the crops were harvested in the autumn. The wheat and millet were brought to the farms and beaten or threshed with wooden tools called **flails,** to separate the seeds from the stems.

Part of the crop was then sent away to pay the farmer's taxes to the emperor. The rest was stored in **granaries**, which were built on stilts to keep the rats and mice out. Pottery models of granaries show that there was sometimes a dog kennel underneath the granaries. Perhaps the dog helped to keep rats and mice — or thieves — away.

The crops were gathered in before winter brought short days. In wintertime not much work could be done in the fields. Instead, the farming families spent their time looking after their animals, mending tools, and making clothes.

◁ Planting rice in China today.

Food and cooking

When people started to settle and to farm the land in China, their diet began to change. Instead of eating meat from the animals they hunted, they ate grains, vegetables, and fruits. They could produce more food by cultivating fields and growing crops than by rearing herds of cattle and sheep to eat. This meant that there was little meat, milk, butter, or cheese in the ordinary Chinese diet. Poorer people ate some meat, from small animals such as chickens, geese, ducks, pigs, fish, and even locusts. Rich people ate meat more often, however, since they had more to choose from, including game. They also ate bears' paws, tiger meat, deer meat, crabs, shrimp, clams, small birds, pheasant, and quail. That the Ancient Chinese people ate monkeys' brains is a myth. However, dog meat was eaten by all the social classes.

In the north people ate millet and wheat. The wheat was sometimes ground into flour to make noodles, but often the grains were eaten whole. Rice was grown in southern China from about 5000 B.C., and after the canals were built during the Sui dynasty, it was also easier to transport to the north of the empire. Vegetables such as onions, Chinese cabbage, bamboo shoots, ginger, and lotus roots were grown, while the fruit crops included peaches, apricots, melons, and persimmons, which are sharp-tasting orange fruits about the size of apples.

Cooking a meal

The stove was a very important part of a Chinese household. It was made of clay and we know from pottery models that it was shaped like a box. There was a hole at one end and fuel was pushed through this to feed the fire inside.

△ Fish was an important part of Ancient Chinese people's diet. Many pictures and models of fish have been found in China. One of the earliest pictures is on a pottery bowl that dates from around 2800 B.C. This model is probably from the Han dynasty and shows that fish was popular then. Some fish were caught in the sea, but the others came from China's rivers and lakes. Sometimes the fish was cooked fresh, but often it was preserved in salt and eaten later.

◁ This bronze wine jar is from the Zhou dynasty. When it was being used, the jar was kept bright and shiny, but it has turned green because it was buried for about 2,000 years. The tongue sticking out of the ox's mouth is the spout, while the tail curls to form a handle. The small tiger standing on the ox's back was used as a knob to lift the flap so the jar could be filled.

When the fire had heated the clay, the food was placed in pots that fitted into holes in the top of the stove. The best pots were made of bronze and were often very elaborate. Some of them were like ordinary saucepans and the food was cooked directly in them. However, the Ancient Chinese were very fond of steamed food, and for this they used a double saucepan. Two pans stood one on top of the other. Water was put in the bottom pan and food in the top one. When the water boiled, the heat from the steam cooked the food in the pan above.

Eating a meal

Food in Ancient China was usually served in a bowl. Bowls that were used every day were made of pottery, but there were also some lacquerware bowls for special occasions. The food was cut up into small pieces before it was cooked, so people did not need knives and forks to eat with. Instead they used chopsticks made from wood or ivory.

△ This patterned lacquerware bowl was found in one of the tombs at Mawangdui in southern central China. It was made during the Han dynasty.

Clothes and appearance

Paintings and pottery tell us a great deal about the clothes and appearance of the Ancient Chinese people. Even more evidence has come from objects found in tombs. The most important find was at Mawangdui, in southern central China, where archaeologists excavated three tombs between 1971 and 1974. These tombs belonged to members of the Da family, who lived during the Han dynasty and were buried between 160 and 150 B.C. One tomb contained a woman's body, which had been wrapped in 20 layers of clothes and then buried inside four coffins. The woman's clothes had been perfectly preserved. They included skirts and robes made of silk, some of which were colored with dyes made from plants, while others had patterns painted or embroidered on them. More clothes were found in other parts of the tomb. There were more skirts and robes, and pairs of flat-heeled shoes, socks, and gloves, all made of silk. Silk was an important commodity at the time and bolts of silk were used as a medium of exchange.

The owner of this tomb was the wife of the prime minister of the province of Changsa, in southern central China, who was very rich. She probably had more clothes than someone from most of the noble families of that time.

Rich men and women in Ancient China wore long silk robes, held in place at the waist with a sash or belt. Men usually wore a hat, but women often went bareheaded. Wealthy women had very elaborate hairstyles that were held in place with long pins and other jewelry. On their feet, both men and women wore boots or shoes made from silk or fine leather. In winter the people kept warm by wearing thicker silk gowns and the furs of squirrels and foxes.

△ This piece of silk cloth dates from A.D. 551.

◁ A pair of silk shoes with turned-up toe caps. The shoes are $11\frac{1}{2}$ inches long, which shows that they date from before the Chinese fashion for foot-binding had begun during the Sung dynasty.

Clothes for the poor

Only rich and noble families wore silk and furs. Everyone else wore clothes made of much cheaper and harsher fabrics. These materials were made from yarn spun from fibers found in the stems of plants. The most common plant was hemp, but some grasses and even a type of nettle were sometimes used. Poor people worked hard for a living, so they needed practical clothes. Both men and women usually wore a short tunic that was tied at the waist, and a pair of trousers that came down to just below the knee. On very cold days they also wore sheepskins.

◁ These farmers' tunics are similar in style to a rich woman's robes, but much shorter. On their feet they wear sandals that are probably made from straw or rushes.

Faiths and beliefs

The Ancient Chinese people had several different faiths. One of these faiths was called Confucianism. It was based on the ideas of a man called Confucius, who was born in 551 B.C. Confucius was China's most famous scholar and thinker. He believed that people were born good, and that they all had a duty to one another. Confucius taught that people should be kind to others and should obey their parents and rulers. He believed that sincerity, courage, knowledge, and sympathy were important. He also taught that everyone had a place in society. Everyone should know what his place was and be content with it. Everyone, from the emperor down to the poorest peasant, should try to live in peace with the world around him. Confucius died in 479 B.C. His students wrote his teachings in a book called the *Analects,* which means "sayings."

Lao Zi and the Way

More than 2,000 years ago, at about the same time that Confucius was teaching, the basic ideas of a belief called Daoism were also being written down. These beliefs were said to have been taught by a man named Lao Zi, who worked in the emperor's library during the Zhou dynasty. However, no one is sure whether Lao Zi really existed. The word "Dao" means "the Way" and it refers to the way in which everything works together in nature. People, animals, plants, sky, and earth are all part of nature. People should think of themselves as no different from any other part of nature. Daoism teaches that if people follow the Way, they may find happiness, health, wealth, and a long life. They will also have many gods, such as, for example, a god of wealth and a god of the kitchen.

△ Confucius in old age. As well as being a thinker, Confucius was also a teacher. He was only 22 years old when he founded his school. Confucius believed that he was passing on wisdom from earlier times to his pupils. He traveled through China to try to convert the rulers to his ways. In later dynasties the study of his writings became very important to the Chinese people.

◁ A Buddhist shrine. Buddhism was brought to China by merchants and monks from India. There were more than 300,000 Chinese Buddhist monks by the eighth century A.D. and many temples and shrines had been built. Buddhists believe that people may have more than one lifetime. In each lifetime they try to live a better life, until they do not need to be born again. They have reached nirvana, or heaven.

Buddhism

Around A.D. 100 the faith known as Buddhism was brought to China from India, where it had begun in the sixth century B.C. It spread across the Ancient China empire, and by the time of the T'ang dynasty, about 1,200 years ago, Buddhism was an important religion in China. In Ancient China, however, no one was forced to follow any one faith. Buddhism existed quite happily with Confucianism and Daoism. These three ways of thinking about life have shaped the Chinese way of looking at the world ever since ancient times.

The importance of ancestors

All Ancient Chinese people respected their ancestors. This does not mean that they worshiped them, but they did not forget them after they died. In the Zhou dynasty, **temples** where the ancestors could be remembered were built. However, in later times Chinese families put up wooden boards with their ancestors' names on them in their homes.

△ Yin and yang. The Chinese believed there were two great natural forces in the world. They called these forces yin and yang. Each force had to balance the other exactly, as they do in the black-and-red central section in the picture. Each force stood for things that were equal but opposite. For example, yang represented light, hills, males, and noise, while yin represented dark, valleys, females, and quiet. The Chinese thought that yin and yang together explained everything that happened in the world.

Funeral customs

The Ancient Chinese believed that there was a life after death. People thought of their ancestors as part of the living family, and their advice was often asked on important family matters. The ancestors were also told what was happening in the family. On special days, such as the important festival called Qing Ming, people gave their ancestors gifts of food. The Chinese were very practical people, however. Although they offered the food to their ancestors, they usually ate it themselves at a special feast afterward.

The Chinese were very careful to choose exactly the right place to bury people. The spirits, or gods, of a place always had to be asked about the burial. There were spirits in every place. Sometimes one spirit belonged to a whole mountain, but sometimes each rock had its own spirit, too. A water spirit might belong to a large river or a small stream. If the spirits were happy with a burial place, good luck would come to the family, or **descendants,** of the dead person.

△ The burial suit of Princess Dou Wan. The suit is made of 2,160 wafer-thin pieces of jade, fastened together with gold, silver, and bronze threads. Jade was used because people thought it would preserve the bodies. However, when this suit was discovered in 1968, the body inside it had crumbled away.

◁ Taishan was one of the holy mountains of the Daoist faith. Some people still go there to make sacrifices to their ancestors. The favorite time is still the Qing Ming festival in the spring. To reach the top of the mountain, people have to climb up 6,293 steps. Some of the steps can be seen in the top left of the picture.

Living forever

Many Chinese people, especially the Daoists, thought a great deal about life and death. They all wanted to live for as long as possible. Some people even thought they might be able to live forever, if only the magicians could mix the right drink, or **potion.** The magic mixture was called the **Elixir of Life,** and many people tried to make it. Sometimes they used poisons such as mercury, which were far more likely to kill people than to make them live forever!

The tombs of the rich

When a poor person died, the family put as many of his or her belongings as they could spare into the grave with the body. It was believed that the dead person would need them in the next life. The families of emperors and wealthy individuals could afford to give much more than poorer people. Rich families dressed the dead person in fine silk clothes before placing the body in a coffin. The coffin was then placed inside first one and then another, all of which were beautifully decorated. The coffins were then put inside a special underground chamber, together with the dead person's clothes, food, drink, cooking pots, lamps, and ornaments made of jade, bronze, and lacquerware. Pictures of everyday life were often painted or carved on the walls of the tomb. Between 3,000 and 4,000 years ago, in the Shang and Zhou dynasties, servants were killed and put in the tomb in order to do all the work for the person who had died. Horses, dogs, and other animals were also killed and buried. However, from the time of the Qin dynasty onward, pottery models were buried instead of real people and animals.

△ Models of dancers and acrobats were made to be buried in Chinese tombs. This model of a dancer was found in a T'ang dynasty tomb.

Pastimes and festivals

Tomb models, which were buried with rich people, tell us about the different sorts of entertainment enjoyed by the Ancient Chinese. Some of these models are of groups of dancers, acrobats, and jugglers, while others show musicians playing and their instruments. Pictures painted on silk, bamboo, and paper also show scenes of women dancing. A book called *The Spring and Autumn Annals,* which was written every year from 722 to 481 B.C., records that people in villages also danced to celebrate good harvests and healthy animals on their farms.

Festivals

People enjoyed entertainment such as music, dancing, and juggling at the various festivals held throughout the year. The most important festival was held at the New Year. It marked the start of the farming year and was often celebrated with processions and kite flying, as well as feasting. After the Chinese had invented gunpowder, at the time of the T'ang dynasty, the New Year and other festivals were also celebrated with fireworks.

▽ These bronze bells were found in 1955. From the inscriptions we know that they all once belonged to the Marquis of Ts'ai, who lived about 2,500 years ago. The bells range in height from $6\frac{1}{2}$ inches to 8 inches and so they all make a different note when struck with a wooden hammer.

◁ Fireworks and processions are an important part of the Chinese New Year festival. It is a great family occasion. At the New Year, everyone becomes a year older. This is because, although birthdays are celebrated, everyone counts his or her age by the number of New Years he or she has seen.

Hunting and playing polo

Poor people in Ancient China went hunting to find more food. However, pictures on the walls of tombs show us that rich Chinese people hunted because they enjoyed the sport. In the Shang dynasty, young noblemen set out in **chariots** to hunt animals such as deer, wild boars, and hares. While an attendant or servant drove the chariot, the nobleman threw spears at the animals he was hunting. When chariots went out of fashion, people hunted on horseback, using bows and arrows to kill their prey. To help them to chase and catch the animals, they took with them dogs, falcons, and, occasionally, cheetahs.

Gambling and board games

Gambling seems to have been popular in Ancient China. People played games of chance and gambled on the results. Poor people found time to gamble, too. They risked their money on the outcome of a cockfight or on the result of a horse or dog race. Board games were popular, too. The wealthy Chinese had plenty of leisure time in which to play board games similar to chess.

△ A model of a polo player from the T'ang dynasty. Paintings and models found in tombs show us that rich people enjoyed playing polo. It was very similar to the game that is played today, and both men and women took part.

Transportation

A document written about 2,700 years ago suggested that there should be five different grades of roads in China. The narrowest were pathways for people and pack animals. There were roadways for narrow wheeled vehicles, and wider roads for other vehicles. Then there were roads wide enough for two vehicles traveling side by side, and finally roads wide enough for three vehicles to pass one another.

The first emperor, Qin Shi Huangdi, wanted better roads than these, however. He wanted his orders to reach every corner of his empire quickly so he forced thousands of people to build the imperial roads. These so-called "fast" roads were made of packed earth and were so wide near the capital that the center lane was reserved for the emperor and his messengers.

Bridges
From the Han dynasty onward, about 2,000 years ago, the growth of trade and the expansion of the empire led to more and more roads being built. Many of these roads had to cross rivers. If the river ran between low banks, a stone or wooden bridge

◁ Oxcarts carried people as well as goods. This model of a cart drawn by an ox was found in a tomb dating from the Han dynasty. It is about 2,000 years old. Oxcarts were not fast forms of transportation, but they could carry very heavy loads.

◁ Emperor Yang Ti cruising on the Grand Canal to celebrate its opening. The royal boat stood 49 feet above the water and had a dragon's head at the front. It was at the head of a procession of boats that is said to have stretched for 62 miles. Some 80,000 laborers were needed to tow the boats, which contained the emperor's wife and family, with all his officials and the members of his court.

could be built across it. Many rivers flowed between steep banks, however, and had to be crossed by bridges that were hung or suspended from strong bamboo poles. By the time of the Sui dynasty, about 500 years later, the Chinese could make high-quality wrought-iron chains. They used these chains to build iron **suspension bridges** that could be made to cross, or span, a river that was up to 328 feet wide.

Water transportation

Traveling by water was often easier than land travel in Ancient China. During the Qin dynasty, about 2,200 years ago, the Chinese rulers began to build canals. These canals made it easier to transport goods to markets to be sold. This meant that trade increased and people with goods to sell became richer. Rich people paid more taxes, which in turn helped to pay for more canals, roads, and bridges.

In the reign of the second Sui emperor, Yang Ti, between A.D. 605 and 618, the Grand Canal was built along the line of an earlier canal, joining the Yangtze River in the south to the Yellow River in the north. This was soon busy with boats called **barges,** heavily laden with rice and other goods, that were towed by forced labor.

△ The Marco Polo Bridge, near Beijing. It was built of stone about 800 years ago and it is supported on 24 arches. At each side there are 140 pillars, each topped with a stone lion and its cubs. Altogether there are 485 lions on the bridge! The traveler Marco Polo visited the bridge about 600 years ago and reported that ten men could ride abreast across it.

Trade

The Chinese people have been involved in trade for at least 3000 years. **Cowrie** shells found in tombs from the Shang dynasty were probably used as money. We know this because at a later date some Chinese states made bronze coins in the shape of cowrie shells. Other bronze coins were shaped like tools, such as spades and hoes. When the emperor Qin Shi Huangdi united China in 221 BC, however, he decided that the empire should have one set of coins. He chose small, round bronze ones and had them cast with a square hole in the middle. This saved bronze and also meant that the coins could be threaded on a string and carried around.

The merchants

Merchants were supposed to be the lowest class of people in China. In Han times they were not allowed to wear silk or ride on horses or to become government officials. The reason given was that they did not make anything themselves, but lived on buying and selling things which other people had made. The real reason, however, was that the emperors feared that the merchants would become too powerful. Giving merchants a low place in society was a way of controlling them.

Eventually, merchants were accepted in Chinese society. Their sons were allowed to become officials and their daughters were thought to be suitable brides for scholars.

Government controls

The Chinese kings and emperors were themselves involved in trade and industry. During the Zhou dynasty, 3000 years ago, horse trading became important. The Chinese had few horses, while their enemies from the north fought on horseback. So

△ A piece of 'spade' money from 550 BC. It is thought that tools were originally bartered for other goods because some of the earliest coins are shaped like them. The later round coins minted in the reign of Qin Shi Huangdi were known as 'cash'. When long strings of cash became too heavy to carry around, they began to be left for safety with people who gave the merchants a paper note in exchange. This was the start of the use of paper money in China.

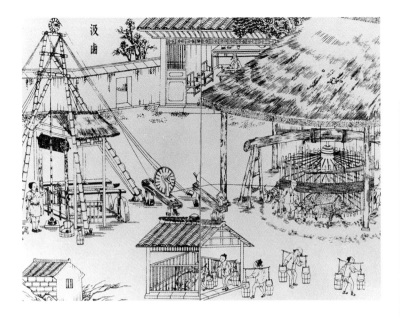

◁ A woodcut showing salt being extracted from the ground in southern China.

Chinese rulers had to rely on trading to exchange goods for horses. The state took control of both salt and iron production and kept all the profits from them. The government also collected heavy taxes on goods at customs posts and in market places.

The silk trade

Silk cloth from China found its way to Europe in the days of the Roman Empire about 2000 years ago. The silk traders travelled mainly along a route called the Silk Road. This was not a paved road, but an overland track which stretched from Chang'an in northern China across many thousands of kilometres to end in Antioch, in what is now Turkey. The Silk Road had many branches, and few traders made the complete journey. Instead, each merchant carried his goods on a train of camels from one city to the next. There the goods were sold or exchanged for other merchandise. Then the trader returned to sell those goods in the first city. Silk also travelled from China by a sea route to India, The Gulf, Egypt and the east coast of Africa. This route was used mainly by Arab traders, who also carried **spices** and pottery from China.

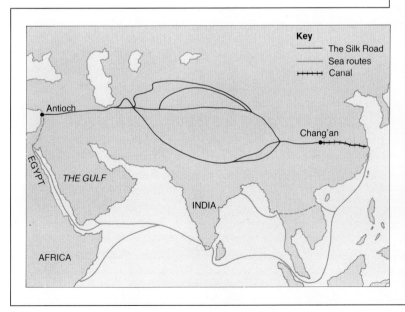

Key
— The Silk Road
— Sea routes
+++++ Canal

Antioch
Chang'an
EGYPT
THE GULF
INDIA
AFRICA

The engineers

Some of the greatest engineering works of the ancient world were carried out by the Chinese. The men in charge of the building projects were either generals in the army or officials of the civil service. They worked under orders from the emperor. The engineers built walls, roads, canals, palaces, and tombs for the emperors. They also worked on **irrigation** projects to bring water to the land to help the farmers, and drainage projects to try to prevent rivers from flooding. Some of these works can still be seen in China today.

Canals

In China the main rivers flowed from west to east, while people and goods wanted to move from south to north. One way of solving this was by sailing along the coast from the mouth of the Yangtze River. However, this piece of coastline was very dangerous. There were strong winds and currents, and there was also danger from attack by pirates. So, in both the Qin and Sui dynasties, canals were built to link the rivers by inland routes.

The Great Wall

By 221 B.C. there were a number of guard walls in north China. The walls were built at different times by different states. Their purpose was to defend the people from the enemies to the north and to defend themselves from one another. About 2,000 years ago, the first emperor, Qin, ordered that all these walls should be joined up and extended. Counting all the twists and turns, this Great Wall was around 4,000 miles long, of which 1,860 miles guarded the frontier. The wall had watchtowers every several hundred yards. The towers had openings wide enough to allow crossbows to be fired at the enemy. It was also possible to signal a warning from one tower to the next, in case of an attack.

The Great Wall was built by soldiers and forced labor, made up of prisoners of war and convicts. As the wall was in a remote area, the workers, their food, and their tools all had to be brought there. To do this efficiently, a massive network of roads was built.

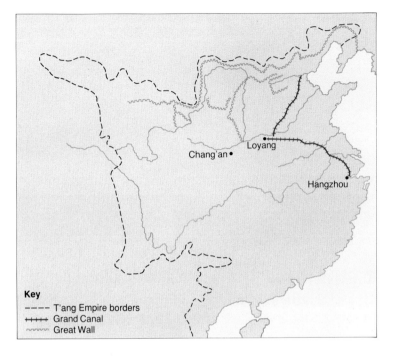

◁ The positions of the Grand Canal and the Great Wall in the T'ang dynasty (A.D. 618–907).

Irrigation and flood control

Sometimes the rivers had too little water, and sometimes too much. To prevent droughts and floods, dams and artificial islands were built.

◁ People are building a dike to contain the waters of a river, which is rising rapidly. The long bundles of brushwood will trap the soil and the loose pebbles. They will strengthen the bank against the force of the water.

39

Many inventions came out of the experience of everyday life. Nobody knows who was responsible for them or when they happened. One of the simplest was the wheelbarrow, which soon became widely used in Ancient China. It meant that one person could easily push a heavy load of up to 220 pounds.

Another invention was the waterwheel. It was used to raise water from rivers to the fields for irrigation and to give power to the bellows that heated furnaces in the iron industry. Another Chinese invention was a horse collar that rested on the horse's chest muscles, not on its throat, and so allowed it to pull vehicles without the risk of choking itself. The Chinese also invented a device called an odometer, which recorded the distance traveled by wheeled vehicles.

Paper making and printing

Cai Lun, who lived about A.D. 105, is often given the credit for inventing paper. In fact, like many other inventions, paper was not the idea of any one

◁ An Ancient Chinese **seismograph.** China has many earthquakes. These can strike without warning, killing people and destroying farms and villages. A court astronomer called Zhang Heng invented the first earthquake detector, or seismograph, in A.D. 132. It was a bronze vase with eight dragons attached to it, and eight bronze toads sitting opposite the dragons. Each dragon had a ball in its mouth. When an earthquake occurred, the dragon facing the center of the earthquake spit the ball out of its mouth and into the open mouth of the nearest toad. In this way the astronomer knew the direction of the earthquake. This picture shows a model of Zhang Heng's seismograph.

person. In Cai Lun's time, it had already been made from mashed silk fibers for about 50 years, but this method was very expensive. Cai Lun experimented successfully with plants and rags, which were mashed with water and then pressed into sheets of paper.

By approximately A.D. 700, the Chinese had also invented printing, using wooden blocks. This made it possible to produce many copies of one book more quickly and cheaply than by hand copying. These extra copies meant that knowledge could spread further.

Scientists

The Chinese discovered magnetic rock, or **lodestone,** sometime before 200 B.C. More than a thousand years later, the scientist Shen Kuo experimented with magnets and wrote about his findings. By the 1180s the Chinese had a compass that helped them to travel long distances by sea. It was called a **maritime** compass. Other scientists, called astronomers, were interested in studying the stars and planets, and others measured time. The Chinese were also good at arithmetic and used a calculator, called an **abacus**.

△ The Ancient Chinese used gunpowder in warfare, as well as to make fireworks. They used it to shoot arrows and to frighten their enemies with noise and smoke. Gunpowder was probably discovered accidentally when an alchemist was trying to make an elixir. He made gunpowder instead and probably singed his beard with the explosion!

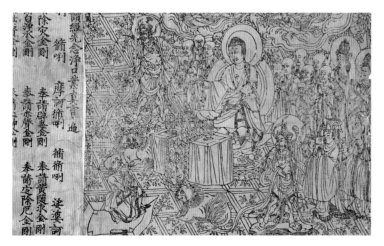

◁ A page from the *Diamond Sutra,* which is a sacred Buddhist scroll. It was printed in A.D. 868 and is the oldest printed text in the world. It is also the first text to have a printed date.

Writing and painting

The first Chinese writing appeared on oracle bones over 3,000 years ago. In early Chinese writing a word was written with a small drawing or character, called a pictogram. This worked well for some words, such as bird, dog, or tree, as it was easy to draw a pictogram for them. It was much more difficult to write words that expressed feelings, such as love. To solve this problem, the Chinese put two pictograms together.

One set of characters

At first people in different parts of China used different pictograms for the same words. When Qin Shi Huangdi came to power in 221 B.C., however, he wanted every person in his empire to be able to understand his orders. To make sure that they did, he said that only one set of pictograms could be used throughout the empire. His close adviser, Li Si, wrote a list of around 3,000 characters that were in use at that time. Everybody had to use these pictograms and the same system is still in use in China today. This means that although people in China may say words differently, for 2,000 years they have read and written the same language.

△ Li Bo, a famous poet of the eighth century. Li Bo was almost as famous for drinking too much rice wine as he was for his poetry. Here he is being helped home by two friends. Li Bo is said to have died when he fell out of a boat. He was trying to embrace the moon's reflection in the water.

◁ A group of scholars meeting in a garden. Scholars and emperors, as well as artists and poets, enjoyed writing, painting, and good conversation. This picture is said to have been painted in the 12th century by the emperor Huizong.

◁ Mountains and water were popular subjects for painting. The mountainsides were usually very steep. If people were shown, they were often very tiny and not at all important.

Writing as an art

In China, writing has always been an art as well as a means of communication. Traditionally it was done with ink brushes, using careful strokes. Painting developed from this method of writing. In many silk scrolls, the writing is as important as the picture.

Chinese paintings

Some of the earliest paintings to survive are more than 2,000 years old. They were painted on the walls of tombs during the Han dynasty. From later times, however, there are paintings on silk, paper, and bamboo. Some show scenes from court life. Others show busy streets and peaceful landscapes.

In landscapes especially, Chinese artists wanted yin and yang to be in balance, as they were in real life. Some yin elements are tortoises, the earth, winter, darkness, and valleys, while some yang elements are dragons, the sky, summer, lightness, and hills. To keep the balance in a painting, an artist might paint a dragon in a valley or a tortoise on a hill. Ancient Chinese artists did not paint exactly what they saw. Instead they painted what they remembered about a scene. In this way they tried to paint the "spirit," or feeling, of a place.

Pottery and porcelain

Chinese archaeologists date the beginning of settled life in China by evidence of farming and by the appearance of the first pottery. This can be dated back to **Neolithic** times, about 10,000 years ago, when the first pots were made by smearing clay inside wooden bowls or baskets. This was left to dry and then baked in a fire to make it hard. Other early methods of making pottery include molding it in the hands from a ball of clay and coiling long strips of clay on top of each other to make larger vessels. Excavations at Longshan in eastern China, between 3000 and 2400 B.C., show that people were using a potter's wheel to shape their pots. However, most early pots had a dull finish and felt slightly rough when they were touched.

During the Zhou dynasty, about 2,500 years ago, the Chinese discovered how to glaze their pots to make them smooth and shiny. The glaze was a kind of melted glass, which was painted on the surface of the pot after the pot had been shaped. When the pot was baked, the glaze became hard and shiny. Minerals containing metal oxides could be added to the glaze to make different colors.

△ This pottery animal dates back to around 2000 B.C. It may have been used as a jug, since liquid can be poured out of its open mouth. From earliest times, the Chinese liked to make their pottery objects as interesting and as beautiful as possible.

Porcelain

The Ancient Chinese discovered how to make **porcelain** about 1,300 years ago. Porcelain is much harder and finer than pottery. It allows light to shine through it, so porcelain is described as being translucent. Porcelain also makes a ringing sound when it is tapped. An Arab writer in the ninth century said that porcelain bowls were "as thin as flakes of glass" and that you could see the glint of water through them. The earliest porcelain has been found in a T'ang dynasty tomb dated A.D. 661.

◁ Princess Yong Tai's model horses were made in a type of three-colored pottery. The colors came from glazes that were painted on the models before they were fired. In the heat the glazes blend and mix together to form new colors. This pottery horse looks very life like. It dates from the T'ang dynasty and was found in the tomb of the princess, near Xi'an.

Making porcelain

To make porcelain, the potter mixed fine white china clay, called **kaolin,** with a mineral called feldspar and another one called quartz. Water was added to make a stiff paste that could be shaped. Once shaped the pot was left to dry. Then it was glazed with a mixture of feldspar, quartz, and just a little kaolin. Then it was fired at a temperature of 2,200–2,500 degrees Fahrenheit. In this very high temperature, the feldspar melted around the particles of clay, making a glassy surface. If the clay was thin, the finished porcelain could be very fine and delicate. When the clay was thick, the pot would be strong and heat-resistant. From the Sung dynasty on, the state controlled some porcelain making.

Porcelain was used throughout China and also exported to other countries. Rich people collected special pieces, but the best pieces of all were kept for the emperor.

△ A fine example of porcelain from the Sung dynasty. Chinese potters probably never left their own country, but their work was well-known and admired in many countries. The word "china" is still used today to describe all sorts of pottery and porcelain.

45

Crafts and metalwork

The Ancient Chinese were very skilled craftworkers who produced beautiful objects from many different materials. Among their finest carvings are objects made from jade. This stone comes in many shades from white to a yellowish brown, but the Chinese prized green jade and white jade most highly. From about 4,000 years ago until the Shang dynasty, jade was made into axes and knife blades. It could be ground into blades with very sharp edges. During the Shang dynasty metal replaced stone for making tools. Jade began to be carved into jewelry and ornaments. It was also used to make sets of musical stones, which gave out mellow notes when they were struck with a stick.

Bronze

Bronze was first made in China during the Shang dynasty, about 3,000 years ago. It was made from a mixture of copper, tin, and lead. To make an object out of bronze, the metalworker, or caster, first had to make a clay mold. This was in several pieces, and could be held together like a hollow jigsaw

△ A bronze monster mask and ring from the time of the first emperor. It was made by the lost wax method. In this, a model would be made from wax and any decorations would be cut into it. Then a mold was made by covering the model with soft clay. A hole was left in the top of the mold. When the clay hardened, hot metal was poured in. This melted the wax. It ran out of the mold and was replaced by the metal, which was left to cool and harden.

◁ One of the oldest jade treasures in China, this small jade buffalo is just over two inches tall. It is part of a collection found in a tomb dating from the Shang dynasty. Other animals in the collection include a bear, a cow, a tiger, a pigeon, and a dragon.

puzzle. Handles, spouts, and legs could be added to the shape. The mold was filled with hot liquid bronze. When this liquid cooled, the mold was carefully taken apart so that it could be used again. Over time bronze reacts to oxygen, one of the gases in the air. The surface changes color, or **oxidizes.** This is why all the Chinese bronzes we see today are mottled green in color.

Iron

Iron working began in China about 450 B.C. It was an important discovery that may have come from the West, where people had been using iron for 1,000 years. Soon wooden plowshares were replaced by iron ones. Because they could dig deeper and turn over hard soil, more land could be cultivated.

Iron was also used to make hard tips on bamboo drills. This meant that the drills could dig deeper into the ground, and salt could be mined from saltwater or **brine** wells underground. Iron cooking pots were made and iron weapons gradually replaced bronze ones.

Lacquerware

The Ancient Chinese people made many beautiful objects decorated with lacquer. This was obtained from the gray, sticky sap of the lacquer tree. When the sap or resin was heated and mixed with oil, it turned black. It was then used to coat wooden and other objects, including ornaments, bowls, boxes, shields, trays, and musical instruments. Several thin coats of lacquer were painted on. Each coat took several hours to dry. When it was hard, it was polished until it was as shiny as glass. The Chinese knew how to add red, gold, and silver to the lacquer.

△ A lacquer stag from the tomb of Marquis Yi at Leiguden, in southern China. The stag had been buried for about 2,400 years when it was discovered in 1978. It is 39 inches high and 23 inches long. Because lacquer can survive quite well in damp conditions, there are many objects from this period. They include food containers, boxes, seats, and tables.

Silk production

The earliest known piece of woven silk cloth to be found in China dates back to around 2700 B.C. It is likely that the Chinese knew how to make silk long before this date, however, since small stone ornaments like silkworms, dating back to 4000 B.C., have been found in northeast China. About 2,500 years later, some oracle bones were inscribed with the characters for silk and silkworm. They also showed the character for mulberry, which is the tree the silkworms live on.

The legend of silk

There are many different stories about how the Chinese learned to make a silk thread that was strong enough to weave into cloth. One story tells how the method was discovered by Hsi Ling Shi, the wife of Huang Ti, who ruled in around 2700 B.C.

◁ Part of a hand scroll that was painted in the 13th century. For many centuries silk making was a secret known only to the Chinese people. The punishment for telling the secret to foreigners was death. The Chinese did not want anyone else to know how to make silk to avoid losing some of their trade.

The king had complained to his gardeners that something was eating the leaves of his mulberry trees. The gardeners found that little caterpillars were responsible. Near the caterpillars were their **cocoons**. Hsi Ling Shi was fascinated by these cocoons. She accidentally dropped one into a bowl of hot water. Before she could get it out, a fine thread started to unwind from it. When several threads were joined together, they were strong enough to be woven.

Raising silkworms

Once the secret of silk had been discovered, the Chinese began to raise silkworms. The worms soon became moths. The moths were then kept in a special house where the warmth, amount of light, and air were all controlled. The farmers used braziers, air-vents, and blinds to do this. The women who looked after the moths tried to get them all to mate at the same time. This meant that the workers would know when all the eggs would be produced and would start hatching the silkworms. When the silkworms hatched, they were kept on bamboo trays and fed on mulberry leaves. These silkworms then spun cocoons. Some of the cocoons were allowed to turn into moths. The rest were plunged into boiling water so that the silk fiber could be unwound.

Making silk cloth

The Chinese reeled several silk fibers together on a wheel to make a stronger thread. They then wove the thread into cloth by hand, on horizontal looms. The weavers could make different thicknesses of silk cloth, from fine gauze to heavy **brocade**. Some silk cloth was also embroidered with silk threads in another color.

△ Embroidered silk found in a tomb of the T'ang dynasty. Silk was also made into scrolls, flags, and banners, as well as clothes. Some of the banners were T-shaped and were placed over coffins. They often had pictures painted on them. The pictures seem to show the journey of the body from this life to the next one.

The early dynasties

Chinese legends claim that the first dynasty to rule over a large area of China was the Xia. Their rule was supposed to have started around 2100 B.C. and lasted until 1722 B.C., when it was replaced by the Shang dynasty. However, no one has yet been able to prove whether the Xia dynasty existed or not, and so the Shang dynasty has to be considered as the first one.

△ A bronze ax head like this one would have been useful as a weapon or a tool. It may have been used during the many wars of the Shang dynasty.

The Shang dynasty

The Shang dynasty probably came to power around 1722 B.C. The names of its kings and queens were written down between 104 and 87 B.C. This was accepted as a true record until the beginning of the 20th century. Then scholars wanted more evidence about the Shang. When the oracle bones were found at Anyang in north China, some of them had names scratched on them. These were studied and confirmed the

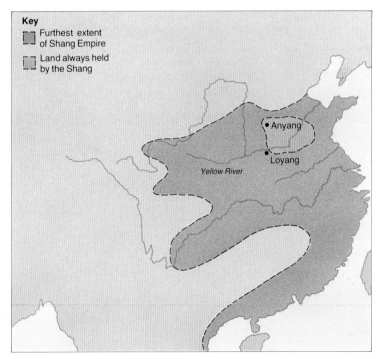

Key

Furthest extent of Shang Empire

Land always held by the Shang

Anyang

Loyang

Yellow River

◁ China during the time of the Shang dynasty, ca.1722–1122 B.C.

existence of 13 of the Shang kings. Archaeologists started excavating at Anyang in 1923. Their work, together with that of later archaeologists, has helped to build up a picture of life in Shang times.

Life under the Shang rulers

During the Shang dynasty, Chinese society was mainly agricultural. At this time, bronze was used to make tools and weapons, as well as ceremonial bowls and cups. Bronze casters and other craftworkers began to live near one another, and gradually towns and cities, such as Anyang, developed. The Shang kings relied on the feudal system to provide them with men to fight their enemies. They also kept many slaves, who were treated harshly. They were often tethered at the neck to keep them at their work and their hands were chained together at night. Many poor workers, the **serfs,** still lived in dugout shelters.

Written Chinese was developed during the Shang dynasty, and many beautiful objects were made from gold, jade, and stone, as well as from bronze. Horse-drawn chariots were invented and were used for hunting as well as in war. The Shang kings made both human and animal **sacrifices** to their ancestors. When a king or a nobleman died, some of his slaves were killed and buried with him, to carry on looking after him in the next life. Others were buried alive.

The end of the Shang dynasty

The Shang dynasty was weakened by wars and rebellions. Even the slaves rebelled against their harsh treatment. When the Zhou army attacked Anyang, many slaves left the Shang army and joined the Zhou. The Zhou won the battle and around 1100 B.C., a new dynasty came to power.

△ The Shang kings had many nature gods. They thought that holding ceremonies and making sacrifices to them would bring good harvests. Bronze vessels were used at these ceremonies to hold wine and food. This jar was probably used to warm the wine for a ceremony.

Toward an empire

The Zhou dynasty lasted for more than 900 years, from 1122 to 221 B.C. It is usually divided into two separate periods. The first was the Western Zhou period, which lasted from 1122 to 770 B.C. The second was the Eastern Zhou, which lasted from 770 to 221 B.C. The Eastern period was also divided into two periods. These were called the Spring and Autumn period, which lasted from 770 to 476 B.C., and the Warring States period, which lasted from 476 to 221 B.C.

The Western Zhou

The Zhou people came from the west of the great bend of the Yellow River. Their way of life was less advanced than that of the Shang people, but they soon adopted many of the Shang ways. The first part of the dynasty was known as the Western Zhou because it had its capital at Hao in western China. The Zhou kings were the first to call themselves the "Sons of Heaven." They believed that they were

△ This bronze mount from a chariot is richly decorated with silver inlay. It was made during the Warring States period. Despite all the fighting, people still found time to make beautiful objects like this.

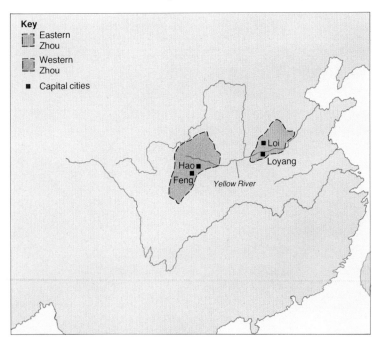

Key
- Eastern Zhou
- Western Zhou
- ■ Capital cities

Loi
Loyang
Hao ■
Feng
Yellow River

◁ The Zhou dynasty and its capitals, ca.1122–221 B.C.

descended from an agricultural god called the
Millet Ruler.

Agriculture was important within the Zhou
kingdom. Most Zhou people were settled farmers
who grew crops. In the high country, the **steppes,**
to the north of the Zhou kingdom, the land was too
dry to grow crops. People here were nomads and
were looked on as **barbarians.** In 770 B.C. they
invaded the Zhou capital of Hao and killed the
king. The next king, Ding, set up his capital at
Loyang, in eastern China.

△ Li Bing was a brilliant
engineer and official. In about
250 B.C. he worked
out a system of canals for
controlling the waters of the
Min River in western China.
Until this time, people
thought the floods were
caused by a bad-tempered
emperor. Li Bing and his son,
Li Er-lang, surveyed the river
and found that the problem
was caused by melting snow.
The Dujiangyan canal system
is one of the greatest early
engineering works in the
world.

Eastern Zhou: the Spring and Autumn period
The Spring and Autumn period in Chinese history
is named after a book that was written at that time.
It was called *The Spring and Autumn Annals* and it
tells the history of the state of Lu, where Confucius
was born. During the Spring and Autumn period,
the production of crops increased, so the nobles
who held land grew richer and more powerful.
They began to fight among themselves.

Eastern Zhou: the Warring States period
The Warring States period started with about 200
small states fighting against one another. This
made life difficult for ordinary people. They had to
pay taxes to pay the soldiers and they lost many of
their crops, which were stolen or trampled by the
armies. They might be conscripted to fight in the
army and risked being killed. As small states were
defeated and taken over, bigger states developed.
Eventually there were seven large states, each led
by men who called themselves dukes. By 221 B.C.
the king of the state of Qin, Qin Shi Huangdi,
controlled all the other states. He brought both the
Zhou dynasty and the feudal system to an end.

Empires and kingdoms

Qin Shi Huangdi became the first emperor of China in 221 B.C. His closest adviser was a man called Li Si, who believed in ideas called "Legalism." These ideas said that people were bad at heart and so they had to be forced to obey the law and the emperor. To make sure that they did, the punishments for disobeying were extremely severe.

The first peasant uprising

When Qin Shi Huangdi died in 210 B.C. his son became emperor. He was not only harsh but weak and greedy as well. In the summer of 209 B.C. he ordered more **conscripts** to the frontiers of his empire. This led to a revolt and a large peasant army was raised. Although it was defeated and its leaders were killed, new leaders came forward. In 206 B.C. the Qin dynasty was defeated and the Han dynasty rose to power.

△ A tiger tally from the Qin dynasty. The first emperor, Qin Shi Huangdi, had tallies made in the shape of tigers. They were made in two halves. The writing on this one reads, "This is the army tally. The right half is with the emperor. The left half is at Yangling." The army could only be taken out on a campaign when both halves of the tally had been presented together. In this way the emperor hoped to make sure that no one could take charge of his army and fight against him.

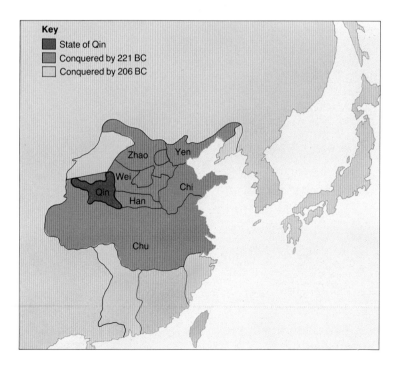

Key
- State of Qin
- Conquered by 221 BC
- Conquered by 206 BC

Zhao Yen
Wei
Qin Chi
Han
Chu

◁ The Qin empire, 221–206 B.C.

The Han dynasty

Although the Han emperors were less harsh than the first emperor and his son had been, they managed to hold the empire together and added new lands to it. During their time, spices, silk, and pottery were carried along the Silk Road or by sea in exchange for gold and jade. Ideas were taken along the Silk Road, too, and by A.D. 100 merchants and monks had brought the Buddhist religion to China. Chinese influence spread to northern Korea and the Han dynasty was not always at peace. There were many rebellions by noblemen as well as peasants. The nomads took advantage of these wars by raiding northern China. In A.D. 220 the Han dynasty was overthrown and the empire started to collapse.

The Three Kingdoms

China was divided into three kingdoms. These were Wei to the north, Shu to the west, and Wu to the south and east. It was a hard time for everybody. The nomads from the north reached the Yangtze River before they were defeated in A.D. 383. This stopped them invading southern China, but the country was divided again. This time there were two main areas of power. The first area stretched from the valley of the Yellow River to the Great Wall, and the second area covered the country from the Yangtze River to the south.

The Northern and Southern dynasties

The invaders from the north soon adopted Chinese ways. At the same time, people who had fled to the south brought the ways of the northern Chinese with them. This kept China united in culture. Fighting and rebellions continued, however. Then in A.D. 581 a new dynasty came to power.

△ This bronze horse was found in a tomb of the Han dynasty. At that time China did not have many horses. However, the Han emperors knew of the fine horses that were bred around Fergana, in Central Asia. The emperors tried to trade with the horse breeders, but they were unsuccessful. So in 101 B.C. the emperor Wu sent an army to Fergana. The army defeated the people and took the horses the emperor wanted.

China reunited

When Wen Ti seized the throne of the Northern kingdom in A.D. 581 he founded the Sui dynasty, which was to reunite China for the first time since the end of the Han dynasty in A.D. 220. Wen Ti sent an army across the Yangtze River and reconquered the south of the country. He also set up irrigation projects. These made it possible to grow more rice and other grain crops and helped to restore wealth to the country. Under Wen Ti's rule, both the amount of taxation and the period of army service were reduced.

Wen Ti's successor was Yang Ti. Under Yang Ti's rule, the examination system for government officials was set up. He spent vast amounts of money on projects such as the Grand Canal and on palaces and pleasure parks for himself. He ordered people to pay ten years' taxes in advance to pay for all this. He also went to war against Korea and was defeated. The peasants started to rebel again and in 618 Yang Ti was killed in an army uprising. Another dynasty had ended.

△ Two pottery models of T'ang princesses. Both pottery and porcelain reached very high standards during the T'ang dynasty. Some pieces show us a lot about the clothes people wore, as well as about the pottery they made.

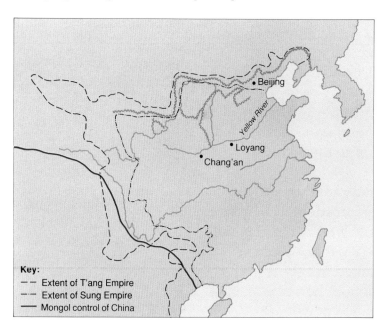

Key:
- − − Extent of T'ang Empire
- − · − Extent of Sung Empire
- ——— Mongol control of China

◁ China reunited, A.D. 581–1279.

The T'ang dynasty

Under the T'ang emperors, **porcelain** was invented and printing was developed. Painting became popular, and the pictures that survive tell us a great deal about everyday life. Pottery figures also show us how people dressed and how they amused themselves. However, like all previous dynasties, the T'ang ended in rebellion and another period of conflict started.

Five Dynasties and Ten Kingdoms

After the T'ang dynasty fell in A.D. 907, five emperors in 53 years tried to reunite China. None of them succeeded, until the first Sung emperor, who came to the throne in A.D. 960.

The Sung dynasty

The first Sung emperor reunited China between A.D. 978 and 979 and brought peace to his people. By the end of the Sung period the population had reached 100 million. However, the north of the empire was still threatened by invaders and in 1126 the Sung dynasty lost control of the whole of northern China. The emperor and his family were captured, but one son escaped. He fled south to Hangzhou and set up the new empire of the Southern Sung.

The Mongol invasion

By the 1230s, the Mongols from the north had conquered the whole of northern China. In 1279 they swept south and conquered the rest of the empire. For the first time the whole of China was ruled by a non-Chinese emperor, Kublai Khan. However, the Chinese way of life, and the system of government that the Chinese emperors had created, remained unchanged until the 20th century.

△ Kublai Khan, the first non-Chinese emperor to rule over the whole of China. He was the grandson of Genghis Khan, who had captured the northern empire from the Chinese in 1279. Kublai Khan brought the Yuan dynasty to power. He ruled China from A.D. 1271 to 1294.

The Middle Kingdom

The Ancient Chinese called their country Zhong-guo, which means "the Middle Kingdom." They used this name for two reasons. China was cut off from the rest of the world by natural barriers. These were the sea, the desert, and the high mountains. These barriers made the Chinese think that their country was the center of the earth. The second reason was that for many centuries Chinese culture was ahead of that of the rest of the world. Apart from jade and the gold they received in exchange for the silk and porcelain they exported, the Chinese wanted little from the outside world. Although they set up cultural links with Korea and Japan, it was Chinese culture that influenced these two countries and not the other way around. Similarly, when people from the north invaded China, they eventually adopted a Chinese way of life, rather than trying to persuade the Chinese people to follow northern people's ways.

For these reasons, there were no great changes in the way the Chinese lived for about 1,500 years, from the time of the first emperor in 221 B.C. to the

◁ Natural barriers, such as the high mountains to the west, helped China to feel cut off from the rest of the world. Even today there are very few roads through these mountains.

◁ A Chinese-style building in Japan. During the T'ang dynasty the Chinese set up cultural and trading links with Japan. Among other things, the Chinese influenced building styles in Japan, but very little Japanese influence reached China.

fall of the Sung dynasty in A.D. 1279. Although there were many rebellions and changes of dynasty, the country was ruled by an emperor and a huge well-educated class of officials. Trade was important, but it was never as important as agriculture. The Chinese allowed some traders to come and buy from them, but they sent few of their own traders out into the rest of the world. Even when people did travel, they did not seem to want to change their way of life; to be more like that of another country. This may have been because of their deep-seated belief in Confucianism and their wish to live in harmony with nature. Their feelings of respect for their parents and their ancestors probably also made them unwilling to change anything.

Until the fall of the Sung dynasty in 1279, this reluctance to change was part of China's strength. In spite of the many rebellions, life there was quite stable. The emperor ruled from his palace and everyone else knew his or her place in life.

△ Some working methods in China have not changed. The people in China today are carrying loads in just the same way as their ancestors would have 2,000 years before them. Even after the fall of the last emperor in 1911, the Chinese relied on people rather than machines to do a lot of the heavy work.

Time line

B.C.

600,000 Early humans are living in parts of China. They are similar to what we call man, but have a smaller brain. They live by hunting and gathering.

400,000 Peking man live in caves at Zhoukoudian. One cave there is occupied for 100,000 years. The people who live in it know how to make fire and how to use very simple stone tools.

28,000 Early humans have been replaced by the true ancestors of man. They also live at Zhoukoudian, but in a different cave. They still live by hunting and gathering.

9000 The caves at Xianrendong are occupied by hunter-gatherers.

6000 The first farmers start settling in the Yellow River valley.

5000 In the north of China the village of Banpo is built. The people are farmers who live in huts of wattle and daub. They know how to make pottery. In the southeast rice is grown in the Hangzhou Bay area.

4000 Stone models of silkworms from this date have been found.

3500 Stone plowshares, or hoes, used in the Hangzhou Bay area. Fine painted pottery made at Yangshao.

3000 Copper mining starts in China. At Longshan, potters start making pottery on a wheel.

2300 Date of the earliest bronze objects found so far. Also the date of the earliest sample of woven silk.

c. 2100 The start of the legendary Xia dynasty.

c. 1700 The start of the Shang dynasty.

c. 1400 The first oracle bones used.

1122 The Shang are overthrown by the Zhou. This dynasty is divided into Western Zhou (1122–770) and Eastern Zhou (770–221). The Eastern Zhou is again divided into the Spring and Autumn period (770–476) and the Warring States period (476–221).

551 Confucius is born.

450 Ironworking starts in China.

221 The state of Qin overcomes all the other states and its leader sets up a new dynasty. He is Qin Shi Huangdi and China becomes an empire under him.

210 Qin Shi Huangdi dies and is buried in a tomb with his army of terra-cotta soldiers.

202 The Han dynasty starts. It lasts until A.D. 220, but there are many rebellions and upheavals during this time.

A.D.

100 Around this date merchants and monks bring Buddhism to China from India.

78	Zhang Heng, inventor of the seismograph, is born.
100	Papermaking is invented. It uses torn up silk and is very expensive.
150	The court official Cai Lun finds a cheaper way of making paper.
220	Fall of the Han dynasty and start of the Three Kingdoms period.
383	Three Kingdoms is replaced by the Northern and Southern dynasties after an invasion from the north.
581	Start of the Sui dynasty, which reunites China.
618	Assassination of Yang Ti, the second and last Sui emperor. He spent a lot of money on himself, but also made great improvements to the Grand Canal. Start of the T'ang dynasty.
661	Date of the earliest porcelain to be found so far.
c.700	The Chinese invent printing by using carved wooden blocks.
701	The poet Li Bo is born.
907	The Tang dynasty is overthrown. A period known as the Five Dynasties and Ten Kingdoms starts.
960	The Sung dynasty comes to power.
978/9	China is reunited under the Sung.

1126	The Sung lose control of northern China. The capital is moved to Hangzhou. This part of the dynasty becomes known as the Southern Sung.
1180	The Chinese use the maritime compass for sea journeys to Arabia and Japan.
1240	By this date the Mongols have conquered the whole of northern China.
1279	The Mongols conquer the rest of China. Kublai Khan becomes the first non-Chinese person to rule over the whole country.

The dynasties

Chinese history is divided into dynasties. Each dynasty is a period of time when one family was in power. When historians do not know the exact date, they put the word circa in front of it. It means "around" or "approximately" and is usually shortened to ca. The dynasties covered in this book are:

Shang	–	c.1722	–	1122 B.C.
Zhou	–	1122	–	221 B.C.
Qin	–	221	–	206 B.C.
Han	–	206 B.C.	–	A.D. 220

Six Dynasties period	–	A.D. 220	–	580
Sui	–	A.D. 581	–	618
T'ang	–	A.D. 618	–	907

Five Dynasties period	–	A.D. 907	–	960
Sung	–	A.D. 960	–	1279

Glossary

abacus: a counting frame with beads on wires

ancestor: someone from an earlier generation — for example, a parent, grandparent, or great-grandparent

archaeologist: a person who tries to work out what happened in the past by finding and studying old buildings and objects

artifact: any object that was made by people in the past

bamboo: a type of giant grass with a hollow, jointed stem. It has many uses and can also be eaten

banner: a long narrow flag, made from material such as silk

barbarian: the Ancient Chinese name for anyone who was not Chinese

barge: a large, flat-bottomed boat used on rivers and canals

brine: a liquid that is a mixture of salt and water

brocade: a stiff silk material with raised patterns woven into it

bronze: a metal made from copper, tin, and lead

census: an official counting of the population by the government

chariot: a horse-drawn vehicle that usually has two wheels and is used in battles

cocoon: a sheath spun by silkworms and caterpillars from which they emerge as moths

conscript: someone who is forced to be a soldier or a worker

cowrie: a shellfish that is related to the snail; or its shell

cultivate: to prepare and use soil for growing crops

culture: a way of life

descendant: a relative who is a member of a younger generation, such as a son or daughter

dynasty: (1) a ruling family; (2) the period ruled by one particular family

Elixir of Life: a liquid that was supposed to prolong life or change any metal into gold

emperor: a very important ruler. His land was called an empire

excavate: to carefully dig up buried objects to find information about the past

feudal system: a system in which poorer people lived on richer people's land in exchange for some sort of service

flail: a tool for threshing corn or rice

gong: the third group of people in Chinese society

granary: a place where grain is stored after the harvest

hemp: a type of plant with stem fibers that can be woven into cloth

Homo sapiens: human beings like ourselves

inscription: a formal message that can be made up of letters, numbers, or patterns cut into a solid surface

irrigation: watering crops by channeling water from a river or lake along pipes or ditches

jade: a hard stone that can be used to make ornaments, jewelry, or tools

kaolin: the fine white clay from which porcelain is made

lacquer: a hard, glossy coating made from the sap of the lacquer tree

legend: a well-known story about the past that is not always true

lodestone: a magnetic type of ironstone that always points to the north

loess: a fine yellow soil that has been blown by the wind. It is very fertile when it has been irrigated

mandate: a wish or command that has to be obeyed

maritime: relating to the sea

merchant: a person who buys goods in one place and sells them somewhere else, often in a different country

millet: a cereal plant that gives a large crop of small seeds

minister: an important member of the government

Neolithic: belonging to the New Stone Age, about 10,000 years ago, when people were beginning to settle and to farm but still used stone tools

nomad: a person who moves around from place to place, usually with flocks of animals

nong: the second group in Chinese society, made up of the peasant farmers

oracle: something that is thought to use mysterious ways to give the right answers to questions

oxidize: a chemical reaction that occurs when some metals are exposed to oxygen

peasant: a person who works the land for someone else

pictogram: a picture that represents a word

plowshare: the part of the plow that cuts into the ground

porcelain: a fine, hard china, baked at a very high temperature

potion: a liquid medicine

sacrifice: to kill an animal or a person as an offering to a god or goddess

scroll: a roll of paper or silk on which there is a painting or writing

seismograph: a machine for measuring the direction and strength of an earthquake

serf: a person who owns nothing and has very few legal rights

shang: the fourth group in Chinese society, made up of merchants

shi: the first group in Chinese society, after the emperor, made up of nobles and scholars

spices: seeds, stems, or leaves of plants used to flavor food — for example ginger, pepper, cinnamon

steppes: a large grassy plain, usually without trees

suspension bridge: a bridge that has a deck suspended by cables that hang between two towers and are anchored at both ends

temple: a place where people worship their gods and goddesses

tributary: a river or stream that flows into a larger river and so becomes part of it

ward: a section of a city, contained within its own walls

Index

agriculture 11
ancestors 29, 30, 51, 59
Anyang 50, 51
archaeology 7, 10, 11, 26, 51
army 19

bamboo shoots 24
Banpo 6, 10, 11
bridges 34, 35
Bronze Age 7
Buddhism 29, 41, 55

canals 35, 38
Chinese New Year 33
Chinese cabbage 22, 24
cities 20
climates 11
clothes 26, 49, 57
compass 41
Confucianism 28, 59
Confucius 28, 53
cooking 10
craftworkers 13

Daoism 28, 30, 31
Diamond Sutra 41

emperor 5, 13, 14
entertainment 21, 32, 57

farmers 22
farms 32
fireworks 32, 41
first emperor 13, 54
fish 24
food 22, 23, 24, 25, 30
foot-binding 17, 27

Genghis Khan 5
ginger 24
gong 13
Grand Canal 18, 19, 35, 39
Great Wall 18, 38, 39, 55
gunpowder 32, 41

Han dynasty 15, 16, 18, 19, 21,
   24, 25, 26, 27, 34, 43, 55
Hangzhou 57
Hao 52, 53
hemp 22, 27

horse-collar 40
houses 10
Huizong, Emperor 42

irrigation 38, 39

jade 30, 31, 46, 51, 55
Japan 59
jewelry 26

Kublai Khan 5, 57

lacquerware 25, 31, 47
Lao Zi 28
leeks 22
Li Si 42, 54
Li Bing 53
Longshan cultures 11
Longshan 44
lotus roots 24
Loyang 53

mandarins 18, 19
Mandate of Heaven 14
markets 20
Mawangdui 25, 26
merchants 36
millet 22, 23, 24
Mongols 57

nobles 13, 16
nong 13

onions 24
oracle bones 8, 42, 48, 50

painting 9, 12, 14
paper 8, 9, 40, 41
peasants 13
Peking man 6
plows 22
porcelain 44, 45, 57
pottery 5, 44
printing 40, 41

Qin 53
Qin dynasty 5, 31, 35, 54
Qin Shi Huangdi, the first emperor
   6, 13, 15, 16, 18, 34, 42, 53, 54
Qing Ming 30

religion 28, 29, 31, 51, 55
rice 22, 23, 24, 35, 56
roads 38

scholars 13
Shang dynasty 5, 12, 20, 22, 31,
   33, 36, 46, 50
shang 13
Shang rulers 51
shi 13
silk 4, 13, 26, 27, 49, 55
silk trade 37
Sung dynasty 27, 45, 57, 59
Sui dynasty 24, 35, 56

T'ang dynasty 9, 29, 31, 32, 39,
   49, 56, 57, 59
taxes 14, 18, 35
terra-cotta army 6, 18
Three Kingdoms 55
tomb models 31, 32, 34, 45
tombs 7, 31, 43
towns 20
trade 36
traders 13
transportation 19, 33, 34, 51

wards 20
waterwheel 40
Wen Ti 56
wheat 22, 23, 24
writing 5, 8, 42, 43

Xia dynasty 5, 50
Xianrendong 4

Yang Guifei 9
Yang Ti, Emperor 35
Yangshao 11
Yangtze River 35
Yellow River 4, 10, 20, 35, 52
yin and yang 29, 43

Zhou dynasty 5, 12, 18, 22, 25,
   28, 29, 31, 36, 44, 52
Zhou 13, 14, 51, 53
Zhoukoudian 6